Squar

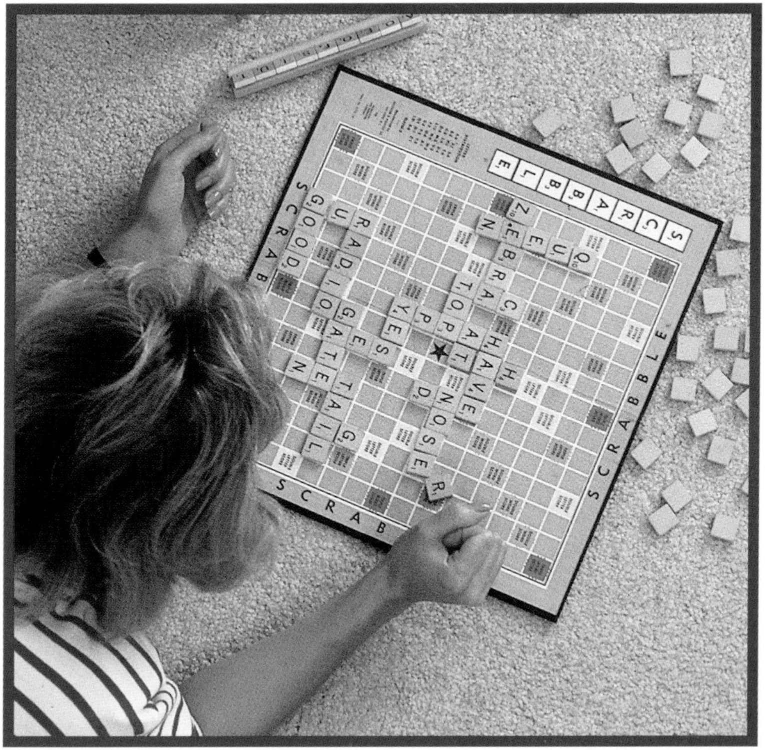

Linda Ekblad

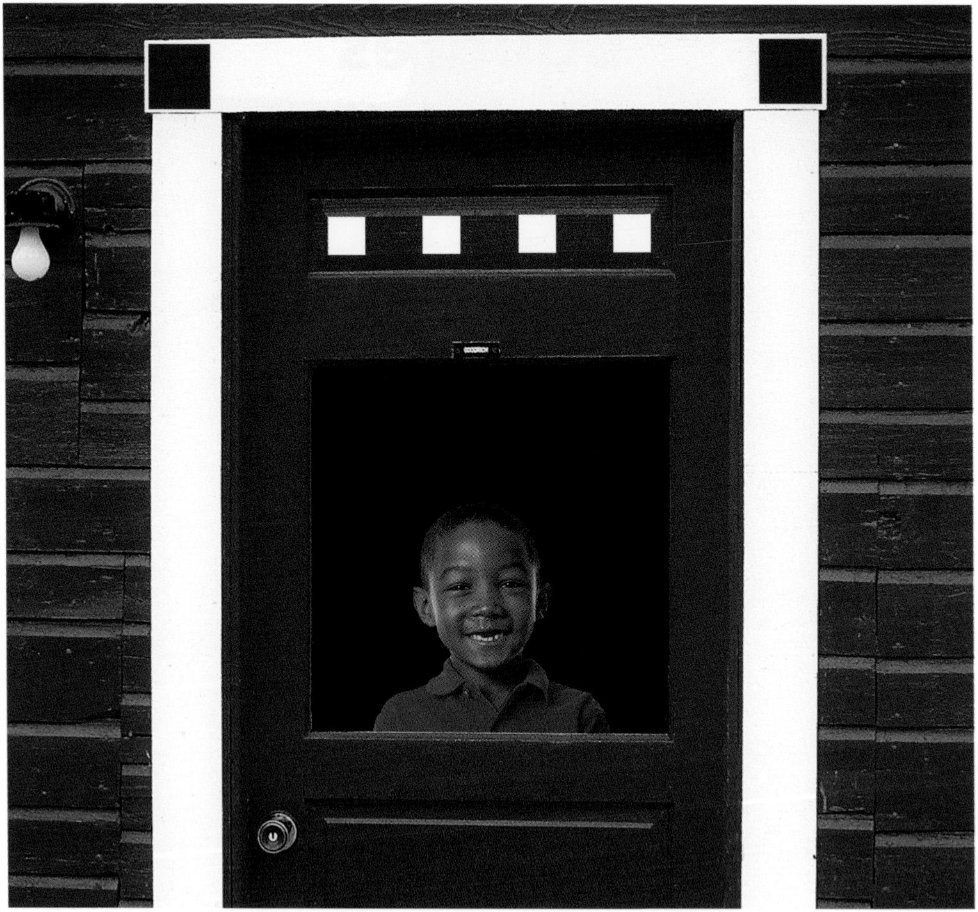

Squares on the door,

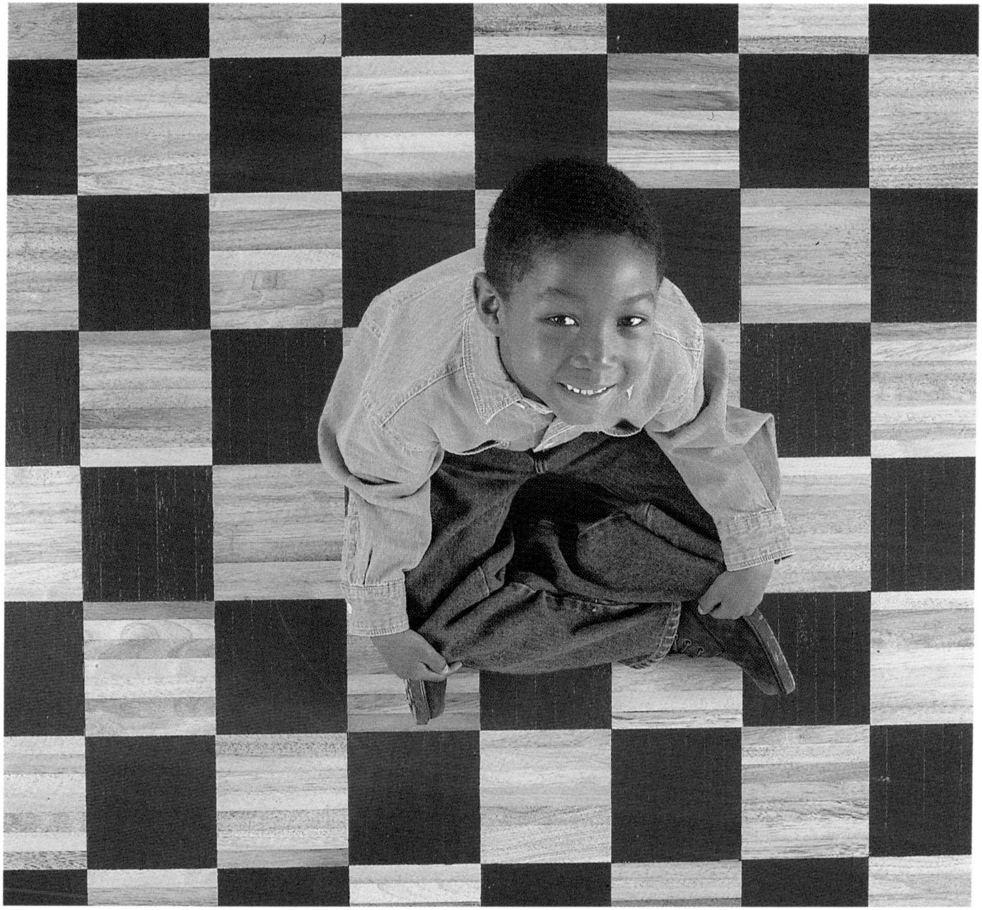

squares on the floor,

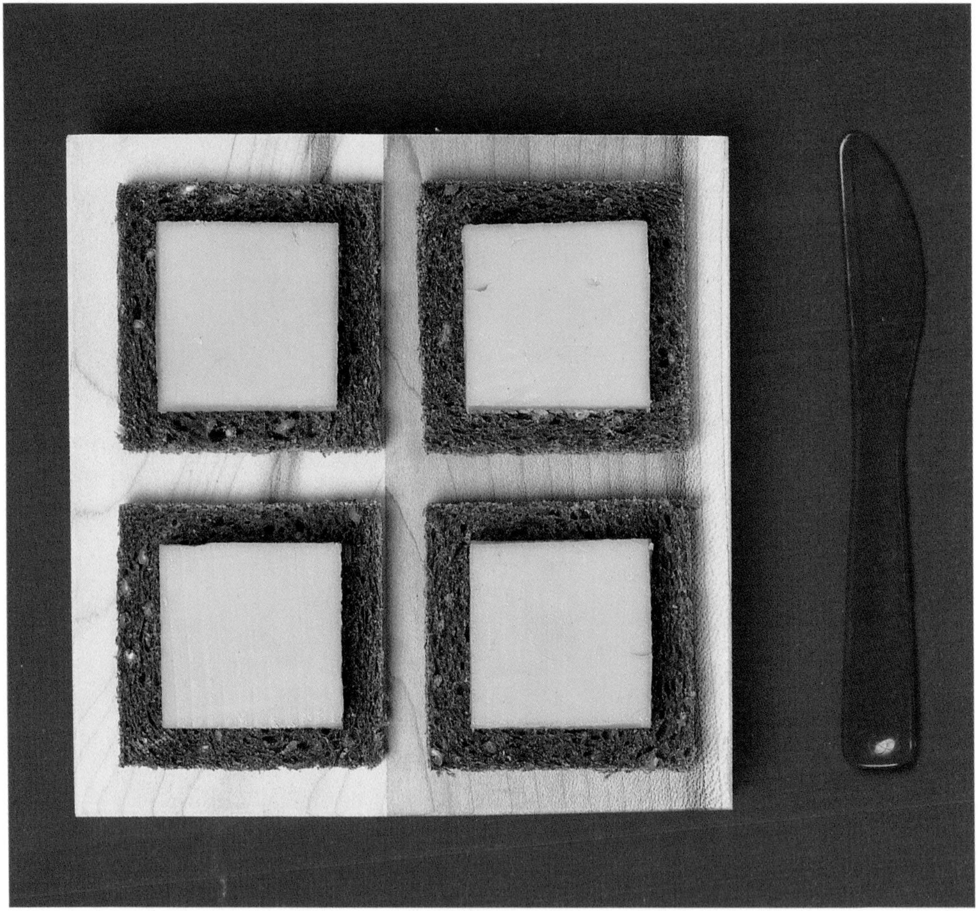

squares to eat,

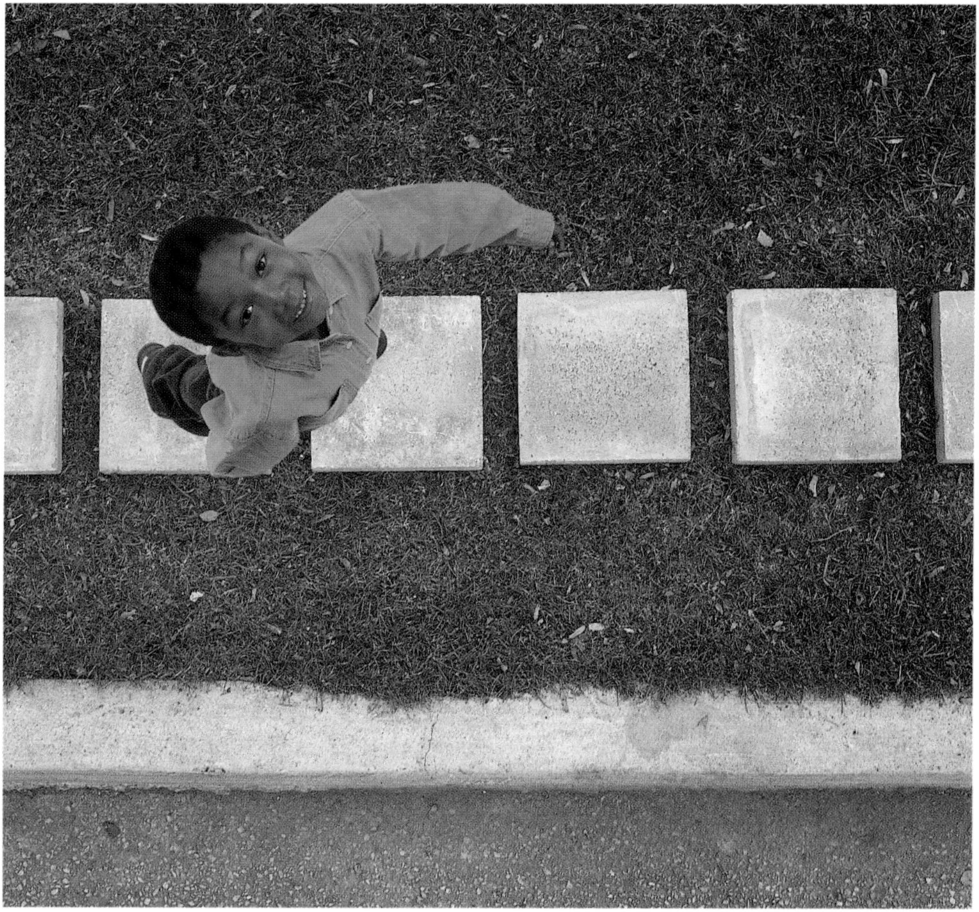

squares by the street,

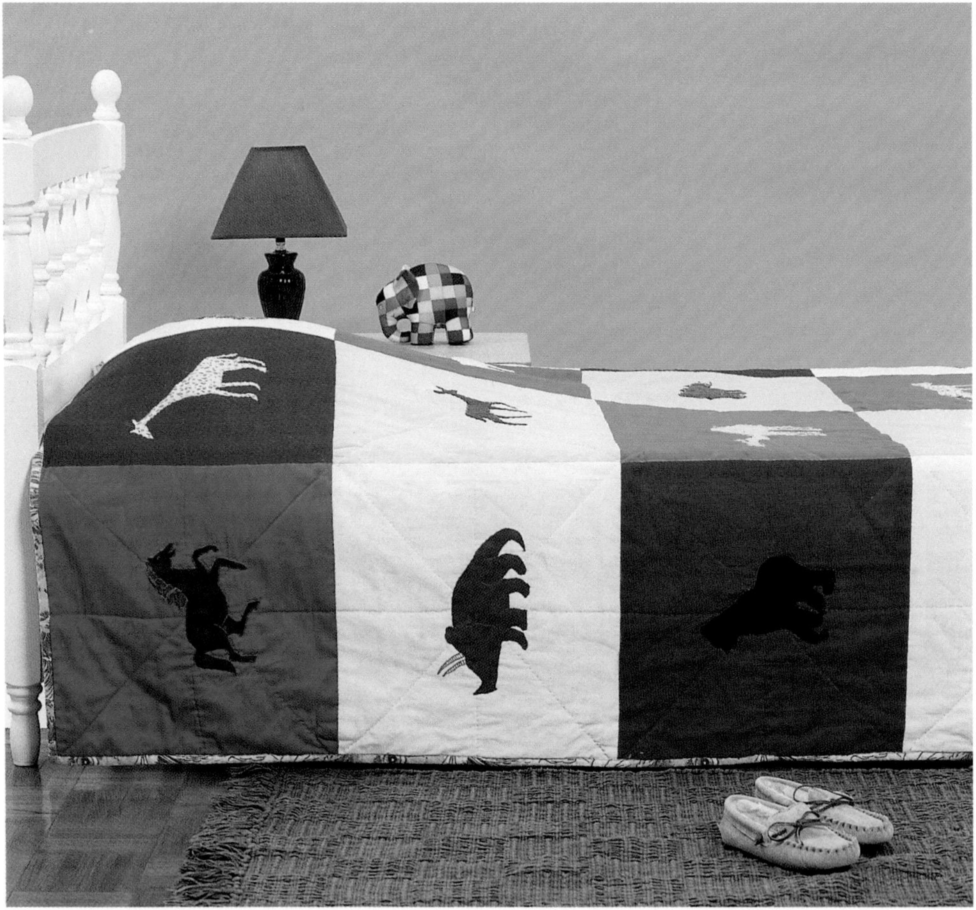

squares on your bed,

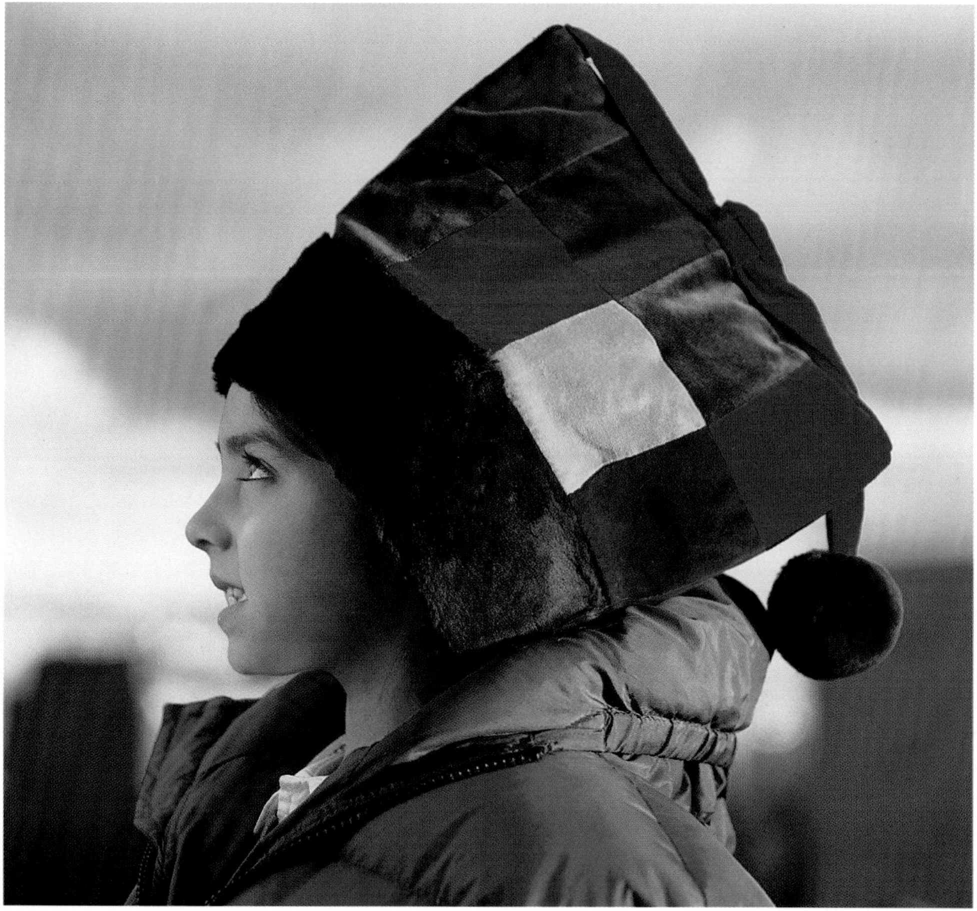

squares on your head,

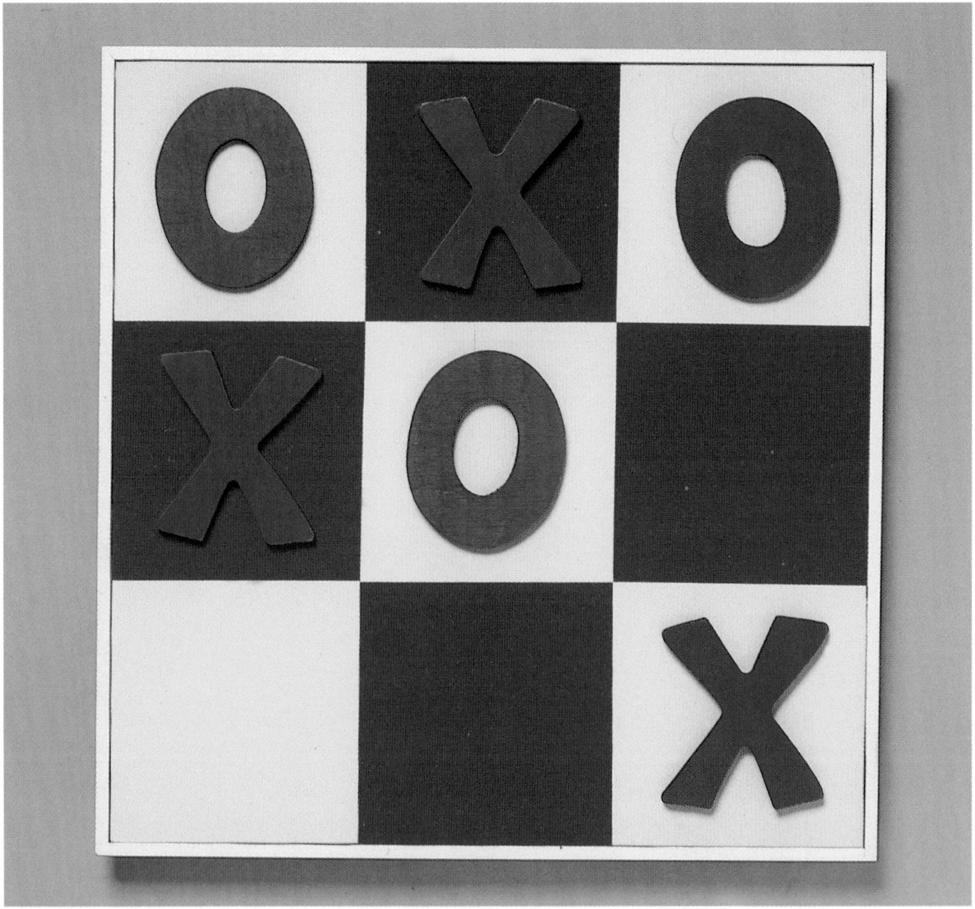

and squares of yellow and red.